BREAKAWAY
STUDY GUIDE

BREAKAWAY

STUDY GUIDE

ANDY STANLEY

Multnomah® Publishers *Sisters, Oregon*

BREAKAWAY
published by Multnomah Publishers, Inc.

© 2006 by North Point Ministries, Inc.
International Standard Book Number: 1-59052-663-5

Cover design by Andrew Cochran at Circle@Seven Studio

Unless otherwise indicated, Scripture quotations are from:
The Holy Bible, New International Version
© 1973, 1984 by International Bible Society,
used by permission of Zondervan Publishing House

Multnomah is a trademark of Multnomah Publishers, Inc.,
and is registered in the U.S. Patent and Trademark Office.
The colophon is a trademark of Multnomah Publishers, Inc.

Printed in the United States of America

For information:
MULTNOMAH PUBLISHERS, INC.
601 N. LARCH ST.
SISTERS, OREGON 97759

06 07 08 09 10—10 9 8 7 6 5 4 3 2 1 0

CONTENTS

Breakaway

by Andy Stanley

Ask children what they want to be when they grow up and the answers are full of heroic images and giant dreams. It's a theme that resides in each of us. Virtually all of us start out with a plan to make an impact somewhere in the world.

But somewhere along the way, life rubs the shine off our dreams. We encounter hardship. Loved ones discourage us. And before long, we acquiesce to a life that's "expected" of us. Until one day we wake up and find ourselves thinking, *This isn't the life I planned. How on earth did I get here?* Maybe there is nothing particularly unpleasant or bad about our lives, but the life we once hoped would be unique and full of adventure is now remarkably just like everyone else's.

That's the point when many of us get restless. We want out. We want to break away from the safe life and its numbing sameness and start all over. We're tempted by the notion that the problem is in the circumstances of our lives; therefore things would get better if we could just change our job, our marriage, our family, or our location. Most of us don't have the courage to actually leave, but we are plagued with a discontentment that begins to eat at us. And even if we don't run away physically, we check out emotionally.

Surely we weren't meant to lead dull, unfulfilled lives that simply check off the years just like everyone else's. Surely we were meant for more.

The good news is that there is indeed a better life. God intended for us to lead lives full of meaning and direction. His intention is to renovate our lives for that purpose. And, yes, we *do* need to break away to find that life. Breaking away does involve change, but the change must take place inside our minds and in our hearts. So if you're ready to accept God's invitation to renovate your belief system, then get ready to experience the breakaway of a lifetime.

A Way Out

None of us begins life hoping to be just like everyone else. In fact, most of us have a distinct fear of being ordinary. We all know what it's like to dream big. As children and teenagers and maybe even young adults, our dreams were larger than life. And that's what made us unique.

But before we knew what was happening, we had jobs, families, and a Palm Pilot filled with long to-do lists. There were homes to buy, cars to wash, and lawns to mow. Little by little, our lives were starting to resemble everyone else's. And our big dreams were nowhere in sight. It's this awareness of the sameness of our lives that can leave us feeling trapped. That's when many of us become deluded by a common misconception. And unless we wake up to reality, we can make the mistake of a lifetime.

In this session, we'll expose a common myth that has been the destroyer of many lives. Just as running away is a bad idea for teenagers, it doesn't work for adults either. If what we ultimately desire is a genuinely fulfilling life, there is a better way. And as we're about to see, it's not so much about changing our circumstances, but renovating the internal belief system that has been driving our decisions.

RUN AWAY

Did you ever attempt to or contemplate running away as a kid? What is it you wanted to run away from? What did you want to run to? In retrospect, why would it have been a very bad idea to run away?

EXERCISE

VIDEO NOTES

(READ THIS OR WATCH SESSION 1 OF THE DVD)

Culture offers an alternative to the sameness in which we find ourselves. Run away! We are sold the message that in order for my life to be better, richer, and more breathtaking, I need to run. I need to break all the rules because it is the rules that are hemming me in. I need to leave my wife, quit my job, move to Vegas.

But ask those who have tried it. At the end of the day, running away only makes life more complicated. Nothing has really changed. You still aren't a rock star, professional athlete, actress, or a super model. You are just you with a bigger pile of regret.

The reason is that although running away might change your surroundings, there is still a common denominator—you. You are where you are because of decisions you made. You believed something at the time of your decisions that led you to think they were either good decisions or bad decisions whose outcomes you could manage. When we get fed up with our outcomes, we assume that if we can just go back and remake some decisions, we will have more pleasant outcomes. But if you alter what you do without altering what you think/believe you will get a similar outcome. This is why second marriages have a higher failure rate than first ones. Deciding different isn't always a solution. If your beliefs about marriage are the same, your choices won't be that different. Changing jobs, husbands, schools, boyfriends, houses, neighborhoods, won't do you any good. A different life outcome is not just a matter of deciding better. It is the outcome of thinking and believing differently.

So in this study we are going to begin the process of renovating our thinking (Romans 12:2), because breakaway thinking leads to breakaway living, which leads to breakaway outcomes. Over the next five weeks we will focus on four core beliefs that, once embraced, have the power to change the trajectory of your life. But before we get to these four core beliefs, we need to take the time up front to examine our current beliefs, decisions, and outcomes.

{ *" The doors we open and close each day decide the lives we live."*
—*Flora Whittemore* }

[NOTES]

_____

_____

_____

_____

_____

_____

_____

_____

_____

_____

_____

_____

_____

_____

_____

_____

_____

_____

_____

_____

_____

_____

_____

_____

DISCUSSION QUESTIONS

Take a few moments to discuss your answers to these questions with the group.

1. What were your dreams in childhood?

2. What are some of the most significant decisions that shaped the outcome of your life?

3. What were the deeply held beliefs behind your decisions?

4. When have you attempted to run away from the outcomes of your decisions? What was the result?

5. If you could change one outcome now, what would it be?

6. Renovating your thinking begins with getting rid of the old. What beliefs do you need to reexamine in order to breakaway in this area?

MILEPOSTS

■ As much as we like to think otherwise, our lives have a sameness that can be stifling and leave us feeling hemmed in and trapped.

■ If I am wondering how my life became the way it is, it is because of the decisions I have made. My decisions are a result of my beliefs.

■ In order to breakaway from the monotony, to rekindle our dreams, we must have breakaway beliefs.

WHAT WILL YOU DO?

Think about an area of your life that is a source of discontentment right now. Have you been tempted to run away? How have your personal decisions gotten you here? What belief was behind those decisions? You may even want to write out the following progression.

My belief that _____ led me to decide to _____ and now the outcome is _____. If change begins at the point of our belief, what brand-new belief needs to replace the old in this scenario?

THINK ABOUT IT

Often we make decisions we know to be wrong because we believe we can manage the outcome. Think of a time you have done that. How did it work? Whether it works every time or not, what assumptions are we making when we do the wrong thing and hope it will somehow turn out right anyway?

CHANGING YOUR MIND

God's Word is the only reliable source from which we can obtain solid truth to fuel a renovated belief system. The break-away life begins here. You can start by meditating on the following verse this week.

"Do not conform any longer to the pattern of this world,
but be transformed by the renewing of your mind.
Then you will be able to test and approve what God's will is—
his good, pleasing and perfect will."

ROMANS 12:2

DAILY DEVOTIONS

To help you prepare for session two, use these suggested devotions throughout the week leading up to your small group meeting.

DAY ONE

Read Romans 12:1–2. Breakaway living begins with breakaway thinking—transforming your mind. Pray today that God would transform your mind over the next several weeks.

DAY TWO

Read Proverbs 3:5. The concept of trust in this culture carried the idea of lying helplessly face down. It is a picture of relying on someone else for security. Why is this often hard for us to do? Evaluate how much you trust God through the day.

DAY THREE

Read Proverbs 3:5 again. Solomon contrasts trusting in God with leaning on our own understanding. Today, observe how often you take things into your own hands rather than trusting God.

Day Four

Read Proverbs 3:6. "Ways" encompasses every arena of life—business, marriage, relationships, conflict management, parenting, money management, etc. Everywhere else in the Old Testament, "acknowledge" is used to signify submission. So in other words, acknowledge His right to rule, say yes to His instruction in every arena. In what areas of your life do you need to acknowledge God. Pick one and focus on submitting to God in that area today.

Day Five

Read Proverbs 3:6 again. Trusting in God will lead you to a lifestyle characterized by good decision-making and positive outcomes. Today, focus on the paths God can lead you to, if you would trust in Him.

LAST WEEK...
We learned that the circumstances (or outcomes) of our lives are shaped by our decisions, and our decisions are ultimately shaped by what we believe. We learned that to live a truly breakaway life, we need to allow God to renovate our beliefs.

God Only Knows

"If only I had known." Those words are full of haunting regrets many of us recognize. We made our decisions and our decisions turned around and made us. We thought our thinking was wise, but time has proven otherwise.

No matter how clever or talented or lucky we are, eventually we must all face the sobering reality that we're not as smart as we think we are. Sometimes the consequences are minimal. And other times they can rip our lives apart. But there in the midst of the painful truth, we will find our first big clue to living a breakaway life.

In this session, we'll explore a simple truth that can mean the difference between regret and satisfaction, frustration and fulfillment. In fact, by learning to follow this principle, you can experience the confidence of knowing that any decision you make will turn out for the best. Because when it comes to making good decisions, it's not how much you know, it's how much you trust the God who knows everything.

OOPS!

Describe a time when a simple miscalculation on your part led to comically bad results. How did it feel to be wrong? Foolish? Embarrassed? Were you able to laugh at yourself?

EXERCISE

VIDEO NOTES

(READ THIS OR WATCH SESSION 2 OF THE DVD)

The first of four breakaway truths is the most basic of all…God knows what's best for you. Now, before you move past this too quickly, stop and think about it. What would happen if you truly believed this? How would it affect your decisions if you really believed that God knows what is best for you in any and every situation? That God knows what will make you happy? That God knows what will make you feel purposeful and alive? That God knows what will fulfill you?

Now, the corollary to this is that God knows what's best for you better than you do. And, before you push back too hard on this, answer these questions. Have you ever made a purchase decision or relationship decision that you thought would add to your happiness/fulfillment/joy that in fact resulted in frustration and anxiety? Have you ever gotten right to the brink of making a decision and something happened so that you didn't get what you wanted? Then you found out later that if you had gotten it, it would have been a disaster? If you have experienced one or both of these, then you know that we don't always know what's best for us.

If ever there was a man who could have trusted his ability to discern what would make him happy and lead to a good outcome it was Solomon. The Bible references him as the wisest man who ever lived. He wrote the books we call the "Wisdom books." And yet, he comes to this very conclusion in Proverbs 3:5–7.

Breakaway living hinges on your answer to these questions: "Who am I going to trust to get me where I want to be?" and "Do I believe that God knows best?" Are you going to continue to trust in yourself? If so, then here's the irony—in your attempt to be different—you are running with the herd. You are leaning on your own limited flawed understanding. That's what everybody does. God has invited you to participate in something far better. He has invited you to break away.

> " *There are two kinds of people:*
> *those who say to God, 'Thy will be done,'*
> *and those to whom God says,*
> *'All right, then, have it your way.'* "
> —C. S. Lewis,
> The Screwtape Letters, 1943

[NOTES]

DISCUSSION QUESTIONS

Take a few moments to discuss your answers to these questions with the group.

1. Has your heart ever misled you into making a
   bad decision? What role did your emotions
   play in that decision? Describe.

2. Looking back on your life, are there any
   decisions you are glad you did not make?

3. Describe a time when you chose God's
   reasoning over your own.

4. Do you agree that God always knows what's
   best for you? Why or why not?

5. In what areas of life is it most difficult to
   choose God's reasoning over your own? In
   what areas is it easiest?

6. What decisions can you make right now
   regarding God's reasoning that will enable you
   to lead a breakaway life?

MILEPOSTS

- Contrary to what most of us believe, we do not know what is best for our own lives.

- God knows what is best for your life.

- If you will acknowledge that God knows best, the outcome of your life will change dramatically.

WHAT WILL YOU DO?

In Proverbs 3:5–6, the words "trust" and "lean" mean the same thing. We are told to trust, not in our own hearts or decision-making abilities, but "in the Lord" or in "his ways." This week as you face each day, begin by affirming this big truth: God knows what is best for you. Imagine that you are literally *leaning* on Him, rather than yourself. How can this truth make a difference in your decisions this week? Are there any specific decisions to be made that can be brought under this truth?

THINK ABOUT IT

It is amazing that a man considered one of the wisest to ever live—Solomon—wrote the words of Proverbs 3:5–6. How does that thought enable you to acknowledge God's wisdom above your own? How does it remind you of His right to rule in your life?

CHANGING YOUR MIND

Because it is so easy to trust in our own wisdom, take time to meditate on this verse throughout the week.

"Trust in the LORD with all your heart and lean
not on your own understanding.
In all your ways acknowledge him,
and he will make your paths straight."

PROVERBS 3:5–6

DAILY DEVOTIONS

To help you prepare for session three, use these suggested devotions throughout the week leading up to your small group meeting.

Day One

Read 1 John 4:9–10. God sent His Son as an atoning sacrifice. He paid a very high price to rescue us from having to pay for our own sin. Why? He valued us. Do you feel like you are valued and loved by God? Meditate today on the fact that the God who created the universe loves *you*.

Day Two

Read John 3:16. For God so loved the whole world. Not just the lovely. Not just those who could do something for Him. God loved. God loves. Each time you see someone today reminder yourself, "God loves them."

Day Three

Read Romans 5:10. God loved us when we didn't love Him. He reached out to us when we were His enemies. Who will you come into contact with today that you would just as soon never see again? Remind yourself, "God loves him. God sent His Son to die for her."

Day Four

Read 1 John 4:11. The proper response to God's action on our behalf is to value those that God values. If you really embrace the fact that Jesus was sacrificed for your sin and the sin of others, then you "ought" to love others. This isn't optional. You are under obligation to love others because of the love He has lavished on you. Who in your life "ought" you to love because of God's love for you and them?

Day Five

Read 1 John 3:18. What can you do today to express your love for those you "ought" to love?

LAST WEEK...

We learned a simple truth: God knows what is best for our lives, and we don't. The breakaway life is one in which we acknowledge this truth about God and submit our decisions and plans to His wisdom above our own.

Red and Yellow, Black and White

Have you ever been in a situation where you felt invisible? You instinctively knew that the people in the office, at the party, or in the conversation, either didn't know you existed or didn't care. You felt marginalized and devalued. Have you ever realized—too late—that you treated someone else in the same way? How we value others determines how we relate to them, and because we don't value everyone highly, we can hurt them and they can hurt us.

If we're completely honest, we tend to value the people around us based upon what they do for us. Whether it's our closest family members, or the people we meet in passing. Sometimes we place value on people because they are valuable to someone we care about. But either way, this is the lens through which we view others: their value to us.

In this session, we'll examine some of the inherent destruction that comes from taking that approach with people. And as we'll learn, there's a better way to evaluate the people around us. In fact, if you will learn to interact with others based on this standard, it will change the direction and quality of all your relationships. So get ready to have your view of others dramatically altered. And in the process, you can escape the predictable ruts that so often take the joy out of relationships.

VIP ENCOUNTERS

Share about an encounter you may have had with a famous or important person. How did you act differently toward that person because of his or her status? Describe how you felt. Nervous? Excited?

EXERCISE

{ *It is the common wonder of all men, how among so many millions of faces, there should be none alike.*
—*Thomas Browne*, Religio Medici }

VIDEO NOTES

(READ THIS OR WATCH SESSION 3 OF THE DVD)

In the rush of the average day, the second truth we will discuss is extraordinarily difficult to keep in focus. But if you did keep it in focus, it would transform every conversation you have. It would put your family, your friends, and your coworkers in a new light. If you embraced this truth, you would never look at anyone the same way again.

The second breakaway truth is that everyone you lay eyes on is someone for whom Christ died. This means that you are surrounded by people of incredible value. The person in the next cube over, the guy who cut you off this morning in traffic, the woman who fixed your coffee, the CEO of the company you work for—God valued each one of them so highly that He sent His Son to die for them.

We have a tendency to value people according to their value to us and treat them accordingly. If I think you can help me...I'll pay more attention. If there's nothing in it for me...what was your name again? We've all treated people that way. We've all been treated that way. We also value the people who are valued by the people we value. Aren't you nice to your boss's kids? Your brother-in-law? Mother-in-law?

Why? Because you value your relationship with your boss, wife, husband…

So in light of this truth, how should you treat somebody who is so valuable to God that He would sacrifice His Son for them? John put two and two together and explained it in 1 John 4:9–11. God expressed His love by sending His Son into the world to die for our sin. He paid a very high price to rescue us. Why? He valued us. All of us. Remember John 3:16? For God so loved the WORLD. Then the proper response to God's action on our behalf is to value those that God values. And that doesn't mean feel a certain way about them. It means act a certain way towards them, "Dear children, let us not love with words or tongue but with actions and in truth" (1 John 3:18).

Everybody you lay eyes on is someone for whom Christ died. This truth is the proper context for every chance encounter and current relationship. Embracing this truth frames every current relationship differently. Your husband, wife, mom, dad, boss, manager, and enemy have intrinsic value to your Creator and Savior. At the cross, God declared us all to be of unparalleled value. Now imagine if we all embraced this simple message and allowed it to permeate the way we treat everybody we lay eyes on. What if we just tried it for a day or a week? What kind of difference would it make?

[NOTES]

DISCUSSION QUESTIONS

Take a few moments to discuss your answers to these questions with the group.

1. Have you ever noticed someone treating you based on the value you represented to him or to her? How did that make you feel?

2. Have you ever changed your opinion about someone based upon his or her connection to someone else?

3. If we value God, how should we see people in light of the fact that God thinks everyone is precious? Give examples.

4. What are the potential consequences if you forget to view the people around you the way God views them?

5. Of all the people God loves, who is the most difficult for you to value?

6. How should your treatment of him or her change as a result of this message?

MILEPOSTS

■ We determine the value of a thing based on what we are willing to pay for it.

■ Every person we have ever come in contact with is of immense value to God, as evidenced by His willingness to pay for them with the death of His Son.

■ Knowing the immeasurable worth to God of those around us will change the way we relate to them.

WHAT WILL YOU DO?

Think back over the past few days and make a short list of the people you encountered. Many you may have passed by without really seeing. Some you may have purposefully ignored. Others may have irritated or angered you. Can you name any of them or describe them? (For example: Betty, our mail carrier, or the red-headed waiter who did such a poor job and got the tip he deserved.) Take a moment to consider the truth that your Savior died for each of the people you have listed. How might that truth change the way you relate to them?

THINK ABOUT IT

In 1 John 4:11 we are told that we "ought" to love others; in other words, we are obligated to love them. Consider the reason behind this "ought." We don't owe it to people to love them because they have done anything to deserve our love. We owe it to them to love them simply because God loves them. This is the basis of unconditional love. How have you based your love for others on their worth in your eyes, rather than God's? Think about the fact that God's love for *you* is unconditional. Take some time to thank Him for His love for you.

CHANGING YOUR MIND

Our value system is often different from God's. That is why meditating on His Word is so necessary. Use this week's verse as a reminder that God values every person you encounter.

"This is love: not that we loved God,
but that he loved us and sent his Son
as an atoning sacrifice for our sins.
Dear friends, since God so loved us,
we also ought to love one another."

I JOHN 4:10–11

DAILY DEVOTIONS

To help you prepare for session four, use these suggested devotions throughout the week leading up to your small group meeting.

DAY ONE

Read 1 Chronicles 29:11. Just because something is in your possession does not mean it is your possession. As you go through the day, every time you see something that is "yours," acknowledge the fact that God really owns it.

DAY TWO

Read 1 Chronicles 29:12. God distributes everything as He sees fit. As you go through the day, meditate on why God has given you the things He has.

DAY THREE

Read 1 Chronicles 29:13. Today, make a list in your mind of all the good things God has given you and thank Him for them.

Day Four

Read 1 Chronicles 29:14. When he recognized God's generosity, David was inspired to be generous towards God. What is your response to God's generosity to you?

Day Five

Read 1 Chronicles 29:11–14 again. How do these verses impact the way that you use money? Today, think about your financial transactions and how these verses should impact them.

Last week...

We learned that <u>everyone</u> we have ever encountered or ever will encounter is valuable to God, so much so that He sent His Son to die for each one. This fact alone is enough to revolutionize every relationship we have.

Avoiding the "Mine" Field

When it comes to breaking away, one of the toughest areas to master is our money. Virtually everyone dreams of being financially free. And yet, statistics show that fewer and fewer people are saving their money. Instead, debt is increasing its hold on the culture. The American Dream is based on financial accomplishments. But ironically, more and more people are living out a financial nightmare.

So what's the key to breaking away financially? Is it making more money? Curbing your spending? Learning how to pick the right mutual funds? According to the Bible, the answer lies a little deeper beneath the surface than those things. While earning and saving are important, God is more interested in our basic attitudes and beliefs about money. And therein lies the key to our much-sought breakaway.

In this session, we'll examine the role our beliefs play in shaping our net worth. If you can learn to leverage this dynamic, everything you think and do regarding money can change. And although we can't give you the winning lottery numbers, you may find a winning perspective to help you break away financially.

MINE!

EXERCISE

Tell about a prized possession from your childhood. Why was it so important to you? What did you do—like using one of those tiny locks on a diary, or booby-trapping your bedroom—to protect your treasure?

VIDEO NOTES

(READ THIS OR WATCH SESSION 4 OF THE DVD)

The third truth is that everything belongs to God. Everything. You may think that just because something is in your possession you own it. But when you think about it, whoever has the right or power to take something away from you possesses ultimate ownership. Your broker knows this. He knows that at any moment you can walk in and take it all back. Every time you pay property taxes you are reminded of this. You don't really own that land. You are just managing it for the county and paying them for the privilege!

David understood this truth and acknowledges it in 1 Chronicles 29:11, "Yours, O Lord, is the greatness and the power and the glory and the majesty and the splendor, for everything in heaven and earth is yours. Yours, O Lord, is the kingdom; you are exalted as head over all."

David also acknowledges a related truth in the next verse. "Wealth and honor come from you; you are the ruler of all things. In your hands are strength and power to exalt and give strength to all." Everything is distributed by God as He sees fit. We think our assets are the product of our hard work and ingenuity. We think we married well. We think we are clever. Those things all factor in, but the inescapable truth is that if God owns it all, then He certainly has maintained control of how it has been divvied up.

The moral of the story is, we are stewards, not owners. A steward is defined as someone who manages someone else's stuff. Think about it this way: When you sit down with good financial managers, one of the first questions they ask you is, "What are your goals?" They make it clear they are looking out for you. You wouldn't think much of the manager who said, "I can't wait to get my hands on your money. I've got my eye on a new boat." Good financial managers realize that when you entrust them with your portfolio, it is not their money to use however they want. Also, a financial planner never feels guilty for handling a lot of money. He feels honored and accountable. The reason you feel guilty is because you think it is yours.

Imagine what would happen if you renewed your mind to this truth? You think, "Oh no! I'll hate life. I'll never get anything new. I'll have to live in a shack." Do you know why that is your first response? Because you don't trust God. You don't think He loves you or wants you to enjoy life. When you embrace this truth, you save more, give more, waste less, and you will find yourself in a better financial situation than you are now. You become more responsible with what you have been given and you make yourself someone who God can trust with more.

> { " *Money is better than poverty,*
> *if only for financial reasons.* "
> —*Woody Allen* }

[NOTES]

DISCUSSION QUESTIONS

Take a few moments to discuss your answers to these questions with the group.

1. What deeply held convictions about money were you raised to believe? What have been the outcomes of those beliefs?

2. Does the suggestion that God owns everything seem relevant in today's world? Why or why not?

3. What emotions do you feel upon hearing the suggestion that God owns everything? Relief? Dread? What does that tell you about your view of God?

4. How do you feel about the truth that everything is distributed by God? How does this truth change your perspective about possessions?

5. What would be the biggest difference in your life if you were to view yourself as a manager of God's money instead of as an owner?

MILEPOSTS

■ Everything we have is God's. He owns it all.

■ We are managers of God's resources.

WHAT WILL YOU DO?

First Chronicles 29:12 lists three resources that are given to us from God: wealth, honor, and strength (or ability). Think of something God has given you in each of those categories. Be as specific as you can.

Wealth:

Honor:

Ability:

According to the truth of God's Word, the things you listed are not yours, but God's. Thank Him for choosing to distribute them to you and take some time to ask Him how you can manage them faithfully and responsibly.

THINK ABOUT IT

Remember one of the first times you gave in such a way that it was a sacrifice? Or do you recall the first time you saved enough to buy something you really wanted? In both instances, parting with your hard-earned resources had an impact on you. What was the outcome in your life when you "let go" of money or a possession? Did you do it as a manager of God's resources?

CHANGING YOUR MIND

Consider writing out this week's verse on a piece of paper and placing it in your wallet or checkbook. Use it as a reminder that everything you are blessed to have is God's.

"Wealth and honor come from you; you are the ruler of all things. In your hands are strength and power to exalt and give strength to all."

I CHRONICLES 29:12

DAILY DEVOTIONS

To help you prepare for session five, use these suggested devotions throughout the week leading up to your small group meeting.

DAY ONE

Read Psalm 33:8. "Fear" is often used in the Bible, not in the sense of being scared of someone, but of being in awe of someone. The psalmist calls everyone in the world to stand in awe of God. Stop periodically today to acknowledge the awesome God we serve.

DAY TWO

Read Psalm 33:9. You would not be here if it were not for God. Nothing would be, and no matter what you believe about God, that simple undeniable truth should cause you to recognize your dependency upon and accountability to Him. Take inventory of the multitude of created things you come into contact with today. Remind yourself that God created them with simply His word.

DAY THREE

Read Psalm 33:10. David, the author of this psalm, was aware that all his power and success as king was only with God's permission. David's plans could be thwarted in a heartbeat. Why are we so confident that we can control outcomes? What are you planning for now that you need to acknowledge your dependence on God for its completion?

DAY FOUR

Read Psalm 33:11. God has a multigenerational plan. He's up to something. He's doing something. What evidence do you see around you today that God is up to something in the world?

DAY FIVE

Read Matthew 11:12. God is up to something, and you are invited to play a part. Today, meditate on the part you could play in God's unfolding plan.

Last week...

We learned the simple truth that God owns everything we have. That means we are simply managers of His resources. Although we tend to think earning and saving are the keys to financial success, we learned that it's more important to understand our role as stewards of God's resources.

Something's Up

In ancient times, people believed that the earth was the center of the universe, and that all other heavenly bodies revolved around our planet. But in the 1500s, a man named Copernicus changed all that. He presented evidence that there was much more going on in the universe than we had ever realized. For starters, he suggested that earth is but one of many planets in our solar system. And the sun is one of many stars in our galaxy. Copernicus was right. And as belief in the Copernican system spread, it changed our understanding of the universe forever.

A similar shift awaits us when we truly open our hearts to God's plan for the world. Like ancient thinkers, we tend to operate as if God created the world to revolve around us. We pray with an emphasis on our needs. We study Scripture in order to improve our lives. And we measure the goodness of God based on the level of ease, comfort, and pleasure He grants us. But when things don't go our way, we get confused. Suddenly, our worldview doesn't make sense. It's as if the planets get out of place.

In this session, we'll get to the core of a belief that can change our entire understanding of life. God is up to something in the world. And it's bigger than anything we imagined before. And once we're ready to embrace this reality, life will start to make much better sense.

CANCELLED!

EXERCISE

Has there been a time in your life when you constructed a plan that fell apart? Describe a time when your plans were, as Psalms 33:10 says, "thwarted." How did you react initially? How did the loss of control feel?

VIDEO NOTES

(READ THIS OR WATCH SESSION 5 OF THE DVD)

The last breakaway belief we will discuss begins with this realization: God is up to something in this world. Now you may push back on this idea because at first glance, it might seem like God is nowhere to be found. You certainly see no evidence of His activity in your office, your home, or on the nightly news. But the fact remains that God is at work behind the scenes, below the surface.

Think about when Jesus walked the earth. There He was, the Savior of the world, God incarnate, buying food at the market, rubbing shoulders with people who were totally oblivious. They were feet away from the long-awaited Messiah and they were more concerned with how ripe the figs were. If you would have asked the Jewish leaders what God was up to, they would have said, "Not much." But God was up to something huge right in front of them, and God is up to something big right now.

Reflect on the words of Psalm 33:8–9. "Let all the earth fear the LORD; let all the people of the world revere him. For he spoke, and it came to be; he commanded, and it stood firm." God created the world. Why? Because He was bored? No. God had a plan and a purpose when He set this world in motion. Read vv. 10–11. "The LORD foils the plans of the nations; he thwarts the purposes of the peoples. But the plans of the LORD stand firm forever, the purposes of his heart through all generations."

God has a multigenerational plan. He's up to something. He's doing something. We are tempted to think God is just up in heaven being God. Watching to see if we behave. Helping us find our car keys. Checking on our church attendance. Not so. He had a reason for creating this world and He has not deviated from it.

That brings us to the second part of our breakaway belief. God is up to something in this world…and you have been invited to play a part. Jesus made it clear in the Great Commission (Matthew 28:19–20) what God is up to in our generation and the part we are invited to play. Basically He has said, "Leverage your words and deeds so that people are drawn to me through you. Then teach 'em what I taught you so that they can teach others." So what will you do? Will you sit on the sidelines or will you choose to be a part of what God is doing in the world?

{ *When a man does not know what harbor he is making for, no wind is the right wind.* }
—*Seneca*

[NOTES]

DISCUSSION QUESTIONS

Take a few moments to discuss your answers to these questions with the group.

1. On a scale of 1–10, how tightly is your life organized around God's plan for the world?

2. In your own words, how would you describe God's plan for the world?

3. What's the best example you've ever seen of someone whose life reflected the belief that God is up to something?

4. What are some unique ways your life could reflect that belief?

5. What obstacles make it difficult for you to break away completely and live such a life?

MILEPOSTS

■ God is up to something in the world.

■ His plan began generations ago and continues for generations.

■ We have been invited to take part in His eternal plan.

WHAT WILL YOU DO?

God's plan is to reconcile people to Himself. He is about the business of drawing men and women—through us—into His kingdom. What can you do to jump into the stream of what God is doing in the world?

THINK ABOUT IT

Think back over the past year. How have you seen glimpses of God's plan working out in and through your life? What evidence have you seen that He is up to something in this world?

CHANGING YOUR MIND

Use the verse this week as a reminder to look for evidence that God is up to something. Ask Him to show you ways to get in on His plan.

"The Lord foils the plans of the nations;
he thwarts the purposes of the peoples.
But the plans of the Lord stand firm forever,
the purposes of his heart through all generations."

PSALM 33:10–11

DAILY DEVOTIONS

To help you prepare for session six, use these suggested devotions throughout the week leading up to your small group meeting.

Day One

Read Jeremiah 17:9. You often hear the advice, "follow your heart." Why is this not the best advice? As you go through the day, take note of where your heart leads you.

Day Two

Read Jeremiah 17:9 again. Unfortunately, we have a terminal condition. There is no permanent cure for our deceitful hearts. They require constant monitoring. How can you check your motives as you go through the day?

Day Three

Read John 8:32. Until you are willing to turn and face the truth, you will continue to deceive yourself. You will never be free. Today, meditate on the power of truth to free you.

Day Four

Read Romans 12:1–2. A renewed mind is a necessary defense against a deceitful heart. Without doses of truth against which our deceit is contrasted, we are lost. How can you continue to expose yourself to truth on a regular basis?

Day Five

Read Romans 12:1–2 again. It is much easier to let go of some bad decisions when we finally face up to the irrational line of reasoning we use to support them. "Then" you will be able to recognize God's will and will be far more prone to approve—accept—it for yourself. Today, focus on stripping away the deceitfulness of your heart and focusing on the will of God for your life.

LAST WEEK...
We found out God is up to something in the world. Not only is He working out a multigenerational plan to build His kingdom, He has invited us to participate in that plan.

Reality Check

By now, you're starting to understand the role our beliefs play in determining the outcome of our lives. As we've seen, our lives are the sum total of the decisions we make. And our decisions are shaped by the things we believe under the surface.

But that's only part of the story. As we're about to discover, there's another force that has power over our choices. And it's actually stronger than our beliefs. In fact, this dynamic often drives us to make choices that contradict everything we believe. Unless we learn to recognize it and disarm it, our decisions will continue to result in undesirable outcomes…no matter what our beliefs.

In this final session, we'll expose an important characteristic of the human race that has the potential to delude our thinking and turn us against our own principles. And no one is immune. But if you're ready to face reality, you can learn to see this truth in every choice you make in life. And you'll be one step closer to living a breakaway life.

WHITE LIES

E X E R C I S E

Tell about a time when, as a child, you told a lie. Why did you tell it? What was the outcome?

VIDEO NOTES

(READ THIS OR WATCH SESSION 6 OF THE DVD)

Thus far we've talked about four big breakaway truths that have the power to change the trajectory of your life. But today we will discuss a tendency that has the power to lock us into a cycle of decision-making that results in the same kinds of outcomes over and over. It is something we see in others almost immediately, but it is difficult to detect in ourselves. Let us start with a little confession.

If we are all honest, we will admit that most of the time we are not on a truth quest. We are on a happiness quest. Feeling good usually trumps truth. This is why our kids ignore our lectures, "Son, the truth is, that's dangerous!" "Dad, I don't care. It's fun." This is why we eat too much, exercise too little, spend too much, and save too little. Knowing the truth is interesting, but not necessarily motivating.

So we make decisions based on getting what we want, then go on a search for a justification. You see, "because I want to," just doesn't work unless you are nine. It may be the primary reason for much of what we do, but we can't tell other people that. "I bought this car because it is safe." No you didn't. "I got this fully-loaded black Hummer H2 because it is safe. I got black because you can't see it as well and so you're not as likely to run into me." Nobody believes that, but eventually we do. Nobody else may believe our lame excuses, but after a while, we deceive ourselves.

Until we are able to unearth and root out our self-deception, it is impossible to break away. Unfortunately, self-deception is a constant problem. "The heart is deceitful above all things and beyond cure. Who can understand it?" (Jeremiah 17:9). Our hearts are prone to mislead, and there is no permanent cure. It requires constant monitoring and constant checks. You can manage it, but you can't cure it.

So breaking away requires large doses of truth. But because of our propensity to lie to ourselves, it also requires an honest look in the mirror. Thus we need to pause long enough to evaluate our decisions based on these three questions:

1. Why am I doing this…really?
2. If someone in my circumstances came to me for advice, what course of action would I recommend?
3. In light of my past experience and my future hopes and dreams, what is the wise thing to do?

It is much easier to let go of some bad decisions when we finally face up to the irrational line of reasoning we use to support them. When we do, we free ourselves up to live breakaway lives.

> " Man has always sacrificed truth to his
> vanity, comfort and advantage.
> He lives...by make-believe.
> W. Somerset Maugham,
> The Summing Up, 1938

[NOTES]

DISCUSSION QUESTIONS

Take a few moments to discuss your answers to these questions with the group.

1. What are some ways we use explanations as smokescreens for doing what we really want to do?

2. Why is it so much easier to choose what we think will make us happy over what is best for us?

3. Why is it so difficult to be honest and face the truth about our motives?

4. In what areas are you most likely to avoid facing the truth?

5. What are some honest statements you can make as you face up to the truth about yourself in those areas?

MILEPOSTS

■ All of us are in the habit of making decisions based on how we feel and deceiving ourselves about our reasons.

■ The Bible says all of our hearts are deceitful.

■ The only way to manage our natural bent toward self-deception is to know the truth.

WHAT WILL YOU DO?

List some of the decisions you have made recently. Be honest about the "reason" you have constructed and the real reason. Let this be a step toward breaking away from deception and moving toward truth. Do any of these decisions need to change in order to follow the truth?

DECISION	"REASON"
_____	_____
_____	_____
_____	_____
_____	_____

REAL REASON	CHANGE NEEDED
_____	_____
_____	_____
_____	_____

THINK ABOUT IT

Jeremiah 17:9 asserts: "The heart is deceitful above all things and beyond cure. Who can understand it?" Is this a difficult truth for you to swallow? If so, why is that? How does this truth about you make you long to be more dependent upon God and his truth?

CHANGING YOUR MIND

Meditate on these words of Jesus this week. You may want to place this particular verse on your bathroom mirror, as a reminder to live in His truth about you.

"If you hold to my teaching, you are really my disciples.
Then you will know the truth,
and the truth will set you free."

JOHN 8:31–32

Leader's Guide

So, You're the Leader...
Is that intimidating? Perhaps exciting? No doubt you have some mental pictures of what it will look like, what you will say, and how it will go. Before you get too far into the planning process, there are some things you should know about leading a small-group discussion. We've compiled some tried and true techniques here to help you.

BASICS ABOUT LEADING

1. **Don't teach...facilitate**—Perhaps you've been in a Sunday school class or Bible study in which the leader could answer any question and always had something interesting to say. It's easy to think you need to be like that too. Relax. You don't. Leading a small group is quite different. Instead of being the featured act at the party, think of yourself as the host or hostess behind the scenes. Your primary job is to create an environment where people feel comfortable and to keep the meeting generally on track. Your party is most successful when your guests do most of the talking.

2. **Cultivate discussion**—It's also easy to think that the meeting lives or dies by *your* ideas. In reality, what makes a small-group meeting successful are the ideas of everyone in the group. The most valuable thing you can do is to get people to share their thoughts. That's how the relationships in your group will grow and thrive. Here's a rule: The impact of your study material will typically never exceed the impact of the relationships through which it was studied. The more meaningful the relationships, the more meaningful the study. In a sterile environment, even the best material is suppressed.

3. **Point to the material**—A good host or hostess gets the party going by offering delectable hors d'oeuvres and beverages. You too should be ready to serve up "delicacies" from the material. Sometimes you will simply read the discussion questions and invite everyone to respond. At other times, you may encourage someone to share his own ideas. Remember, some of the best treats are the ones your guests will bring to the party. Go with the flow of the meeting, and be ready to pop out of the kitchen as needed.

4. **Depart from the material**—A talented ministry team has carefully designed this study for your small group. But that doesn't mean you should follow every part word for word. Knowing how and when to depart from the material is a valuable art. Nobody knows more about your people than you do. The narratives, questions, and exercises are here to provide a framework for discovery. However, every group is motivated differently. Sometimes the best way to start a small-group discussion is simply to ask, "Does anyone have a personal insight or revelation he'd like to share from this week's material?" Then sit back and listen.

5. **Stay on track**—Conversation is the currency of a small-group discussion. The more interchange, the healthier the "economy." However, you need to keep your objectives in mind. If your goal is to have a meaningful experience with this material, then you should make sure the discussion is contributing to that end. It's easy to get off on a tangent. Be prepared to interject politely and refocus the group. You may need to say something like,

"Excuse me, we're obviously all interested in this subject; however, I just want to make sure we cover all the material for this week."

6. **Above all, pray**—The best communicators are the ones who manage to get out of God's way enough to let Him communicate *through* them. That's important to keep in mind. Books don't teach God's Word; neither do sermons or group discussions. God Himself speaks into the hearts of men and women, and prayer is our vital channel to communicate directly with Him. Cover your efforts in prayer. You don't just want God present at your meeting, you want Him to direct it.

We hope you find these suggestions helpful. And we hope you enjoy leading this study. You will find additional guides and suggestions for each session in the Leader's Guide notes that follow.

Leader's Guide
Session Notes

SESSION 1—A WAY OUT

KEY POINT

Our lives can become mired in routine and sameness the longer we live. Perhaps we started out with big dreams, but our daily responsibilities can make those dreams seem like distant memories. Many of us feel trapped in a meaningless existence that is just like everyone else's. How do we break away from the pack, so that the direction and trajectory of our lives are different? It begins with a renovation of our belief system.

EXERCISE—RUN AWAY

This exercise will likely elicit some laughter. It is fun to reflect on our thought patterns from childhood. Talk with the group about the way children think and how some of that carries on into adulthood.

Notes for Discussion Questions

1. What were your dreams in childhood?
   Everyone has at least one answer to this question. We all can look back to a more innocent
   time when we wanted to be or do something
   significant. Give some time for the group to
   capture what it was like to be a child and
   dream big dreams. Talk, not just about what
   you each wanted to be when you grew up, but
   how you viewed life.

2. What are some of the most significant
   decisions that shaped the outcome of your life?
   It may be helpful to have each person list two
   or three milestone decisions to get the discussion going. Marriage, job, a major in
   college, a move, a decision to follow Christ or
   to obey Him for the first time...all of these and
   many more are possible answers to this question. If your group is talkative, you may
   encourage each person to share one decision
   and the outcome that resulted.

3. What were the deeply held beliefs behind
   your decisions?

   This may require much more thought.
   Encourage honesty, even if it means saying, "I
   don't know." Watch for "aha" moments. It may
   be that someone has never considered the
   belief system that supports his or her decisions. This will be a theme each week, so it
   may take a few sessions for this truth to sink in.

4. When have you attempted to run away from the
   outcomes of your decisions? What was the result?

   Be ready for some tough answers. If someone
   in your group is grappling with the aftershock
   of a divorce or a failed relationship or business, this may be a difficult thing to admit. Be
   ready to encourage honesty without judging.

5. If you could change one outcome now,
   what would it be?

   You may want to mention that everyone has
   regrets. How a person answers this question
   may be the clue to where this study will most
   dramatically impact his or her life.

6. Renovating your thinking begins with getting rid of the old. What beliefs do you need to reexamine in order to break away in this area? This will take some thought. Again, the idea that our beliefs are the first and primary place for renovation may take some getting used to. Encourage the group to discuss beliefs that are common to many of us if it is difficult to share personal experiences.

WHAT WILL YOU DO?

The goal of this assignment is to identify the progression Andy mentions: Beliefs lead to decisions; decisions lead to outcomes. This progression will be part of the structure of every session, so it is important to grasp. Encourage the group to consider this assignment honestly.

THINK ABOUT IT

When we make choices that we know to be unwise or even wrong, and still hope to control the outcome, we are basically playing God. We are operating under an illusion of control. We may not be aware that we do this, but these questions will hopefully challenge our thinking.

DAILY DEVOTIONS

Don't forget to point out that there are optional daily devotions that the members can complete for the next session. These devotions will enable them to dig into the Bible and to start wrestling with the topics that will come up next time.

SESSION 2—GOD ONLY KNOWS

KEY POINT

The simple truth in this session can be approached from two vantage points, and it is likely the people in your group have experienced both. We may believe we know best for our own lives and it is hard to imagine anyone knows better, even God. Or we may have suffered the consequences of our own bad decisions, and we are keenly aware that we aren't wise enough to run our own lives. Either way, it is foundational to the rest of this series to understand this truth: God knows best.

EXERCISE—OOPS!

Almost everyone enjoys telling or hearing a "most embarrassing moment" story. The point of this exercise is to introduce (through the door of humor) the idea that we really don't know what's best for our own lives. Keep it light and fun. The honest examinations will follow.

NOTES FOR DISCUSSION QUESTIONS

1. Has your heart ever misled you into making a bad decision? What role did your emotions play in that decision? Describe.

   Hindsight is a great teacher. Allowing your group to share past mistakes is a good way to delve into a very present truth: We don't know best, God does. So many people heed the advice, "Follow your heart." This question will hopefully cause those who live by that creed to suspect their own hearts.

2. Looking back on your life, are there any decisions you are glad you did not make?

   Again, the point here is to examine our own hearts and discover that they are not reliable. Sharing mistakes that almost happened gives us a breathtaking view of just how far our hearts could, if given full rein, lead us down the wrong path.

3. Describe a time when you chose God's
   reasoning over your own.
   This can be a turning point in your discussion.
   It may be that only a few people share, but the
   stories can offer a window into the wisdom of
   God. The focus here is on Him and His all-
   knowing ability to direct our lives, not on the
   person who chose to follow Him.

4. Do you agree that God always knows what's
   best for you? Why or why not?
   Here is where you, as a leader, can lead the way
   by creating an atmosphere of honesty. Allow for
   answers that reflect a resistance to or struggle
   with today's message. Remind the group that
   the purpose of the group is to examine truth
   honestly. This is an excellent time for the group
   to listen well and encourage.

5. In what areas of life is it most difficult to
   choose God's reasoning over our own? In what
   areas is it easiest?
   While some in your group will share areas
   where they are genuinely striving to know and

follow God—their relationships, finances, direction, etc.—some may share the one area that makes this truth so difficult to swallow. This will give you, the leader, a clue into that person's needs and points to pursue in discussion with them individually.

6. What decisions can you make right now regarding God's reasoning that will enable you to lead a breakaway life?

Don't skip this question! It is easy to discuss this truth in the theoretical realm and totally miss the actions that will make the truth come alive in your life. Encourage the group to share, perhaps in pairs, a specific action step. They may need to consider this a question to ponder over the next week.

WHAT WILL YOU DO?

This assignment is basically a restating of question 6 in the discussion questions. The visual image of leaning from one support to another more sturdy, reliable one may be helpful to some in the group.

THINK ABOUT IT

Admitting that we don't know what's best for our own lives is often very humbling, especially for those of us who are self-sufficient and seemingly strong. Realizing that Solomon, of all people in Scripture, knew how desperately he needed God's wisdom in his own life, can help even the most proud understand.

DAILY DEVOTIONS

Don't forget to point out that there are optional daily devotions that the members can complete for the next session. These devotions will enable them to dig into the Bible and to start wrestling with the topics that will come up next time.

SESSION 3—RED AND YELLOW, BLACK AND WHITE

KEY POINT

Everyone struggles with relationships. Everyone. This week's lesson is startlingly simple, but has immense potential to change our relationships for the better. Imagine everyone in your group, including you, believing that each person they encounter this week is someone for whom Christ died. Imagine the difference applying this truth could make!

EXERCISE—VIP ENCOUNTERS

Most of us would say we are not prejudiced, racist, or social snobs, but all of us tend to value others according to all the wrong standards. This exercise can be fun. The "famous" person does not need to be all that famous. The point is that we don't truly understand the value God places on each and every person. If we did, our relationships would be transformed.

NOTES FOR DISCUSSION QUESTIONS

1. Have you ever noticed someone treating you based on the value you represented to him or to her? How did that make you feel?

   Depending upon the makeup of your group, these answers may range from mildly irritating stories to deeply hurtful ones. Be sensitive to this possibility. It may be that someone in your group has experienced the pain of being treated badly because of his or her social status or disability.

2. Have you ever changed your opinion about someone based upon his or her connection to someone else?

   Often spouses or children of "important" people experience this. Again, be sensitive to the fact that this may represent pain for some in your group. For others, it may simply mean you get to hear some humorous stories.

3. If we value God, how should we see people in light of the fact that God thinks everyone is precious? Give examples.

Hopefully this can be the question that sparks some "aha" moments. The truth that God values everyone enough to die for each and every person is probably not new to the people in your group, but when we begin to think of the individuals we see every day in light of this truth, it becomes real in a new way.

4. What are the potential consequences if you forget to view the people around you the way God views them?

How honestly your group answers this question depends on the group. Answers can be general and predictable or you may be able to probe and help people to answer more truthfully. If this lesson has impacted you, so that you are realizing the need for a change in how you view and treat certain people, share that with the group.

5. Of all the people God loves, who is the most difficult for you to value?

Everyone has at least one "irregular person;" someone who is difficult to get along with or even hard to love. You may need to make sure the group is careful about sharing too honestly if it is possible others may know the person mentioned. This is a good time to share this answer as a request for prayer.

6. How should your treatment of him or her change as a result of this message?

Now may be a good time to make the distinction between how we feel toward others and how we act. It is not hypocrisy to act loving even during those times when we don't feel that way. Again, the decisions we make about our treatment of others can be based on our beliefs, not our feelings.

WHAT WILL YOU DO?

The truth of this week's message will become a reality as it is lived out with people. Those people have names and faces. It is so easy to theorize about love, but much more challenging to really love real people. This exercise will help those in your group make the truth real and active, especially those who like to stay in the theoretical.

THINK ABOUT IT

"We love because he first loved us" is a humbling fact. As we comprehend God's love for us, we will become more convinced of the "oughtness" of loving others. It takes a lifetime to learn to love as God does: unconditionally. Although we may grasp the truth that God values others enough to have died for them, our value system is mired in the conditional. Basking in his love for us takes us a long way in the process of renovating our value system.

DAILY DEVOTIONS

Don't forget to point out that there are optional daily devotions that the members can complete for the next session. These devotions will enable them to dig into the Bible and to start wrestling with the topics that will come up next time.

SESSION 4—AVOIDING THE "MINE" FIELD

KEY POINT

What does it mean to live a breakaway life financially? It means fully embracing the fact that God owns everything. This truth has the power to transform the way you view and use your resources. It can bring about revolutionary change.

EXERCISE—MINE!

From the beginning, the idea that we own what we own is ingrained in us. This exercise is designed to point out that simple fact. If your group includes a lot of young parents, they may want to answer this question using their own children as examples. Either way, the message is clear.

NOTES FOR DISCUSSION QUESTIONS

1. What deeply held convictions about money were you raised to believe? What have been the outcomes of those beliefs?
   This should prompt some interesting discussion in your group, because all of us view

money and possessions based, at least in part, on what we learned growing up. Encourage the group to look beyond the habits they were taught to the beliefs behind those habits. For example: "My family saved and never spent because they believed money was a nonrenewable asset."

2. Does the suggestion that God owns everything seem relevant in today's world? Why or why not? This question is meant to be answered on a feeling level. Encourage those in your group who are struggling with the truth taught today to share openly. God's truth often seems irrational at first, so it is important to work through the jolt this truth causes. For a new follower of Christ or someone who is seeking, "today's world" may seem to make more sense. The affirmation of the rest of the group that God's truth indeed makes the best sense may provide the balance needed in the discussion.

3. What emotions do you feel upon hearing the suggestion that God owns everything? Relief? Dread? What does that tell you about your view of God?

This question scratches beneath the surface of the previous one and gives an opportunity for someone who is struggling to share openly how they feel in that struggle. You may want to share your own initial feelings about how you have felt when you learned a new or difficult truth.

4. How do you feel about the truth that everything is distributed by God? How does this truth change your perspective about possessions?

The truths in today's lesson are so simple and perhaps even familiar, it may be tempting for your group to give stock, "Sunday School" answers to these questions. Probe and prod a bit to make sure your group is thinking about this truth as a reality, not just a platitude.

5. What would be the biggest difference in your
   life if you were to view yourself as a manager
   of God's money instead of as an owner?

   There may be those in your group for whom
   this elicits a very specific answer. For others,
   this is more of a paradigm shift. Make sure
   there is ample opportunity for both kinds of
   answers. Depending on the group, it may be
   that some can share a time when this truth
   caused them to break away from old patterns
   to handle their finances in an entirely new way.

WHAT WILL YOU DO?

This is an assignment to count your blessings...with a twist.
Encourage the group to take the time to do this and to
come up with some specific answers. Just as last week's lesson made more sense when considered in the light of real
people, this week's lesson makes more sense as we consider
the real "stuff" we have.

THINK ABOUT IT

Giving and spending—two aspects of managing God's resources—create an outcome in our lives. The outcome may be both positive and negative. We may choose to give away something, only to experience some regret. But the same action may produce a profound satisfaction as well. The fact that God owns it whether we give it, spend it, or keep it, can change how we view the outcome.

DAILY DEVOTIONS

Don't forget to point out that there are optional daily devotions that the members can complete for the next session. These devotions will enable them to dig into the Bible and to start wrestling with the topics that will come up next time.

SESSION 5—SOMETHING'S UP

KEY POINT

God is up to something. That may be true, but most of the time, we just don't see it. But the truth is: God is not only up to something in the world, He has invited us to be a part of His plan and purpose.

EXERCISE—CANCELLED!

Chances are, everyone in your group will have a fresh example to share of this common frustration. We all know what it's like to plan well, only to have our plans detoured or even demolished. Most of us have experienced this on some scale; from a rained out birthday party to a hurricane-leveled home. Sharing our stories provides tangible examples of how fragile our plans are.

NOTES FOR DISCUSSION QUESTIONS

1. On a scale of 1–10, how tightly is your life organized around God's plan for the world? Be sure the group understands that this is not a "check-up" question designed for you to

measure everyone. It is simply a discussion/
thought starter. Most of us would have to be
honest and admit that our lives are more geared
toward our own happiness than God's plan.

2. In your own words, how would you describe
   God's plan for the world?
   The previous question begs this follow-up
   question. Andy alludes to God's ultimate plan
   in the video. God's heart is to bring others into
   a relationship with Himself. It is important to
   keep this in mind when answering this question. Otherwise, it would be easy to think being
   a part of God's plan means attending meetings,
   being on committees, etc.

3. What's the best example you've ever seen of
   someone whose life reflected the belief that
   God is up to something?
   Take the time to listen to the stories or examples
   shared. This may be a time of inspiration for the
   group. As you hear about people who have
   dared to live their lives believing God is at work

in the world, you will be challenged to live the same way.

4. What are some unique ways your life could reflect that belief?
Again, this can prove to be an inspiring time. Encourage your group to dream and to dream big. Note how varied and unique the responses to this question may be. Remind the group that this is basically a brainstorming session, not a planning meeting!

5. What obstacles make it difficult for you to break away completely and live such a life?
You may want to point out that most of the obstacles have roots in our beliefs. Probe to find out what beliefs are embedded in the obstacles presented.

What Will You Do?

God's plan involves people. As we join him in reaching the very people he has designed us to touch, we get our most poignant and clear pictures of His plan. Even if this exercise surfaces just one person in the life of each member of the group, it is a major step toward each one becoming involved in God's plan.

Think About It

This is essentially an invitation to praise God. Encourage the group to sit and soak in this exercise a bit, to step back and admire God. He is worthy of our admiration and our awe.

Daily Devotions

Don't forget to point out that there are optional daily devotions that the members can complete for the next session. These devotions will enable them to dig into the Bible and to start wrestling with the topics that will come up next time.

SESSION 6—REALITY CHECK

KEY POINT

Excuses, excuses. We all make them. The problem is, while no one else believes our excuses, we deceive ourselves so thoroughly that we believe them. It is because we aren't completely honest about what is really in our hearts that we aren't always able to live the breakaway life. Once we begin to be honest about our motives, we can allow God to work inside us to renovate us completely.

EXERCISE—WHITE LIES

This tendency to put a positive spin on our motives is inbred in each of us. Someone once said, "Children are born knowing how to lie." This exercise can be funny, but it points to that uncomfortable truth: We lie to ourselves and to others.

NOTES FOR DISCUSSION QUESTIONS

1. What are some ways we use excuses as smokescreens for doing what we really want to do?
   Andy gave quite a few examples to get the
   group started. If the discussion starts off slow,
   you may want to ask if anyone can relate to
   the examples in the video. Since this is a uni-
   versal tendency, it shouldn't be a hard
   question to answer!

2. Why is it so much easier to choose what
   we think will make us happy over what
   is best for us?
   This question may lead to a discussion of some
   deep theological issues, such as the sin nature.
   While that is fine, be sure to keep the group
   focused on their own lives and what they know
   from experience to be human nature.

3. Why is it so difficult to be honest and face
   the truth about our motives?
   Again, there are theological answers to this
   question and there are common sense

answers that spring from personal experience. You may want to approach this question from both angles.

4. In what areas are you most likely to avoid facing the truth?

Here is where the discussion can become more personal. Each person in the group may have a very different answer. Some may experience areas of frustration, but some may have deep, hurtful issues, such as an addiction or a sinful relationship.

5. What are some honest statements you can make as you face up to the truth about yourself in those areas?

The answers to this question are the first step in a truly breakaway life. This is essentially the act of confession. Be sure to encourage any member of your group who is honest about a particular issue for the first time. Although it may seem painful, remind him or her that this is the first step in a total renovation.

WHAT WILL YOU DO?

This assignment can be altered to meet the needs of each person in the group. For those who are new to faith, it may be that they need to isolate one area of their lives (instead of making a list of several areas) in which their decisions haven't been honest ones. For others, making a list can be an exercise in restoration.

THINK ABOUT IT

As long as we hang on to a sentimental hope that our hearts are true and good, we will follow them into one bad decision after another. There may be those in the group for whom this is a new truth. For them, there may be a need to grieve as they change their fundamental belief about their own heart. This truth—that our hearts are deceitful—is vital to grasp if we are to breakaway to the life God designed for us to live.